AF270458

BASEBALL
THEN AND NOW

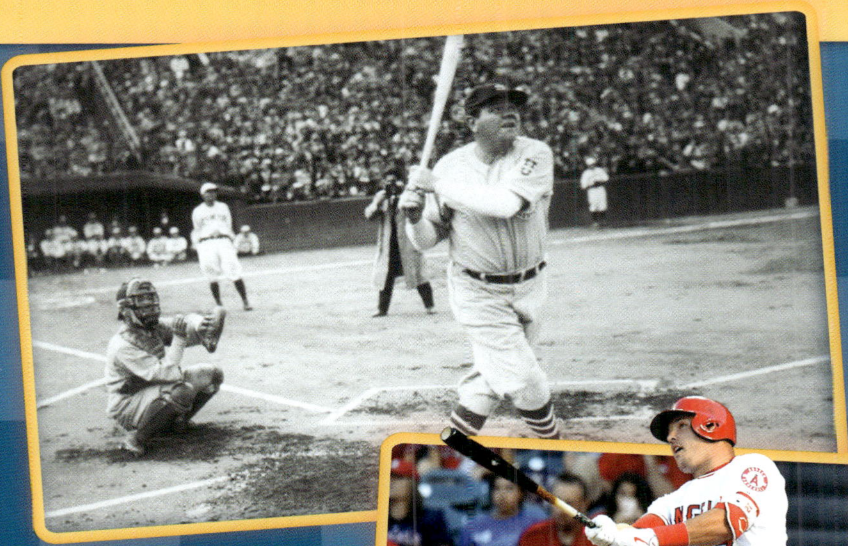

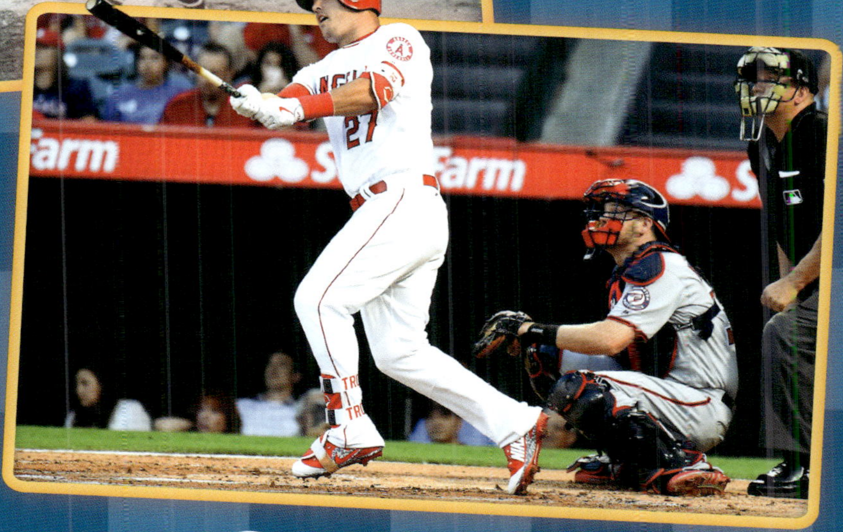

Abdo & Daughters
MIDDLE GRADE NONFICTION

An Imprint of Abdo Publishing
abdobooks.com

R.L. Van

ABDOBOOKS.COM

Published by Abdo Publishing, a division of ABDO, PO Box 398166, Minneapolis, Minnesota 55439. Copyright © 2024 by Abdo Consulting Group, Inc. International copyrights reserved in all countries. No part of this book may be reproduced in any form without written permission from the publisher. Abdo & Daughters™ is a trademark and logo of Abdo Publishing.

Printed in the United States of America, North Mankato, Minnesota

102023

012024

THIS BOOK CONTAINS RECYCLED MATERIALS

Design: Kelly Doudna, Mighty Media, Inc.

Production: Denise Hamernik, Mighty Media, Inc.

Editor: Liz Salzmann

Cover Photographs: Getty Images (both)

Interior Photographs: Alamy Stock Photo, p. 19; AP Images, pp. 4–5, 6, 18, 25, 27, 28–29, 30, 35, 37, 45; Getty Images, p. 1 (both); iStockphoto, p. 7; Library of Congress, pp. 14, 22, 32, 36; Mighty Media, Inc., pp. 3, 42–43; Shutterstock Images, pp. 8–9, 26, 38–39; Wikimedia Commons, pp. 10, 11, 12–13, 15, 16–17, 20, 21, 23, 24, 31, 33, 34, 40, 44–45

Design Elements: iStockphoto

LIBRARY OF CONGRESS CONTROL NUMBER: 2023939285

PUBLISHER'S CATALOGING-IN-PUBLICATION DATA

Names: Van, R.L., author.

Title: Baseball: then and now / by R.L. Van

Other title: then and now

Description: Minneapolis, Minnesota : Abdo Publishing, 2024 | Series: Americana | Includes online resources and index.

Identifiers: ISBN 9781098291754 (lib. bdg.) | ISBN 9781098278656 (ebook)

Subjects: LCSH: Americana--Juvenile literature. | Baseball--Juvenile literature. | Sports--History--Juvenile literature. | History, Modern--Juvenile literature.

Classification: DDC 973.0--dc23

TABLE OF CONTENTS

The Polo Grounds stadium was rebuilt three times. The fourth and last one (*pictured*) was home to the New York Giants from 1911 to 1957.

Chapter 1

THE CATCH

It's the top of the eighth inning in the first game of the 1954 World Series between the New York Giants and the Cleveland Indians. The game is being played at the Giants' home field, the Polo Grounds in New York City. Giants center fielder Willie Mays stands in the outfield, ready to spring into action if the ball comes his way.

Mays has had a great season. He batted in 110 runs and hit 41 home runs. He played in the All-Star Game over the summer. But helping his team win the World Series is what is important now.

The game is tied 2–2. There are no outs and Cleveland has runners on first and second base. Giants pitcher Don Liddle throws a pitch to Vic Wertz. Wertz hits the ball. Later he said, "It was the hardest ball I ever hit in my life." In most parks, it would be a home run. But the Polo Grounds' center field is deep, and the soaring ball stays within the field.

Mays takes off running. If he can't catch the ball, Cleveland will probably score two runs, maybe even three. He keeps his eyes on the ball as he sprints. Near the very edge of the field, he catches the ball over his shoulder. Wertz is out!

But Mays isn't done yet. He whips around so fast his cap falls off. He throws the ball to second base, preventing one runner from advancing and the other from scoring. The crowd stands and cheers.

An Incredible Play

Thanks in part to Willie Mays's catch, the New York Giants ended up winning the first game of the 1954 World Series. They went on to sweep Cleveland and win the World Series. Mays's amazing play went down in history as "the Catch." Many people consider it one of the best plays in the history of baseball—a history filled with exciting, game-changing moments.

Willie Mays was named National League Most Valuable Player for the 1954 season.

Watching and playing baseball are long traditions in the United States. Collectors trade baseball cards and signed balls. Fans eat ballpark snacks, stand for the seventh-inning stretch, and reach for foul balls. Old and new baseball traditions continue to strike nostalgia, patriotism, and excitement in the hearts of Americans.

In the United States, baseball isn't just any sport. It's a uniquely American sport. Over the years, it's both reflected and influenced the country's history. From its American roots and its power to bring Americans together, to its impact on American culture, baseball is associated with Americana more than any other sport.

In addition to photos of players, baseball cards also provide fans with statistics and facts about the players.

Baseball was first referred to as
America's "national pastime"
in December 1856 in a New York
newspaper called *The Sunday Mercury*.

Chapter 2

AMERICA'S PASTIME

Today, America's most watched sport is football. Yet baseball is still known as America's national pastime. Baseball as we know it today was invented in the United States. It was the first professional sport in the United States too. But there are reasons beyond these simple facts that people rally around baseball as the national pastime.

A Powerful Legend

Long ago, many Americans wanted to have a sport they could claim as their own, rather than one adopted from another country. In the early 1900s, a myth spread. People believed that an American man named Abner Doubleday had invented baseball in 1839. This myth helped make baseball seem to be the uniquely American sport people were looking for.

However, Doubleday actually had nothing to do with the invention of baseball. In fact, games similar to baseball had been played in other countries for many years before 1839. Despite Americans' wish for a purely American game, baseball was likely based on the English games cricket and rounders. Cricket had been played since the 1500s and rounders since the 1700s.

But people loved the story that Doubleday invented baseball. Doubleday had served in the Union Army during the Civil War. The idea that the game was invented by an American hero was much more exciting than the idea that it evolved from an English game.

Although baseball's origins aren't purely American, it grew into an all-American game. It was American children and adults across the country who created their

Abner Doubleday retired from the army in 1873. He died in 1898.

own variations of the English games. The New York version became the most popular. It eventually evolved into the baseball of today.

Common Ground

Baseball's status as America's pastime also comes from its history of bringing Americans together. Many immigrants living in New York City were eager to play the sport. Some middle- and working-class baseball clubs made this possible for them. Meanwhile, cricket and other sports were played mostly by wealthier people. Baseball helped many immigrants fit into their new country.

During the Civil War from 1861 to 1865, many Union soldiers played baseball in their free time. Soldiers from New York taught others their style of baseball. Many soldiers and even newspaper reporters attended organized games.

The earliest known use of the term *baseball* is in the children's book *A Little Pretty Pocket-Book.* The book was published by English publisher John Newbery in 1744.

In the South, many people weren't as familiar with the New York style of baseball. But the war exposed them to the game. When the war ended, soldiers from both sides brought the New York style of baseball home. The game spread farther around the country. The North and South had a common game to play after the war. It became a symbol of the united country. As a sport shared by two once-divided parts of the United States, baseball had truly become a national pastime.

Baseball in Hard Times

America's past is overflowing with heroic figures and groundbreaking accomplishments. But dark times have filled many pages in its history

too. Atrocities like war, discrimination, internment camps, and more caused much suffering for people in the United States and beyond. While no game could make the suffering disappear, many people turned to baseball during these dark times.

In the 1800s and 1900s, the United States government took many American Indian children from their parents. It forced the children to attend boarding schools to forget their own cultures and languages and assimilate into white American culture. As part of this, the students were taught to play baseball. Many students ended up using baseball as a way to have fun and escape the oppression of the boarding schools. Students could find a sense of pride in their teams and accomplishments.

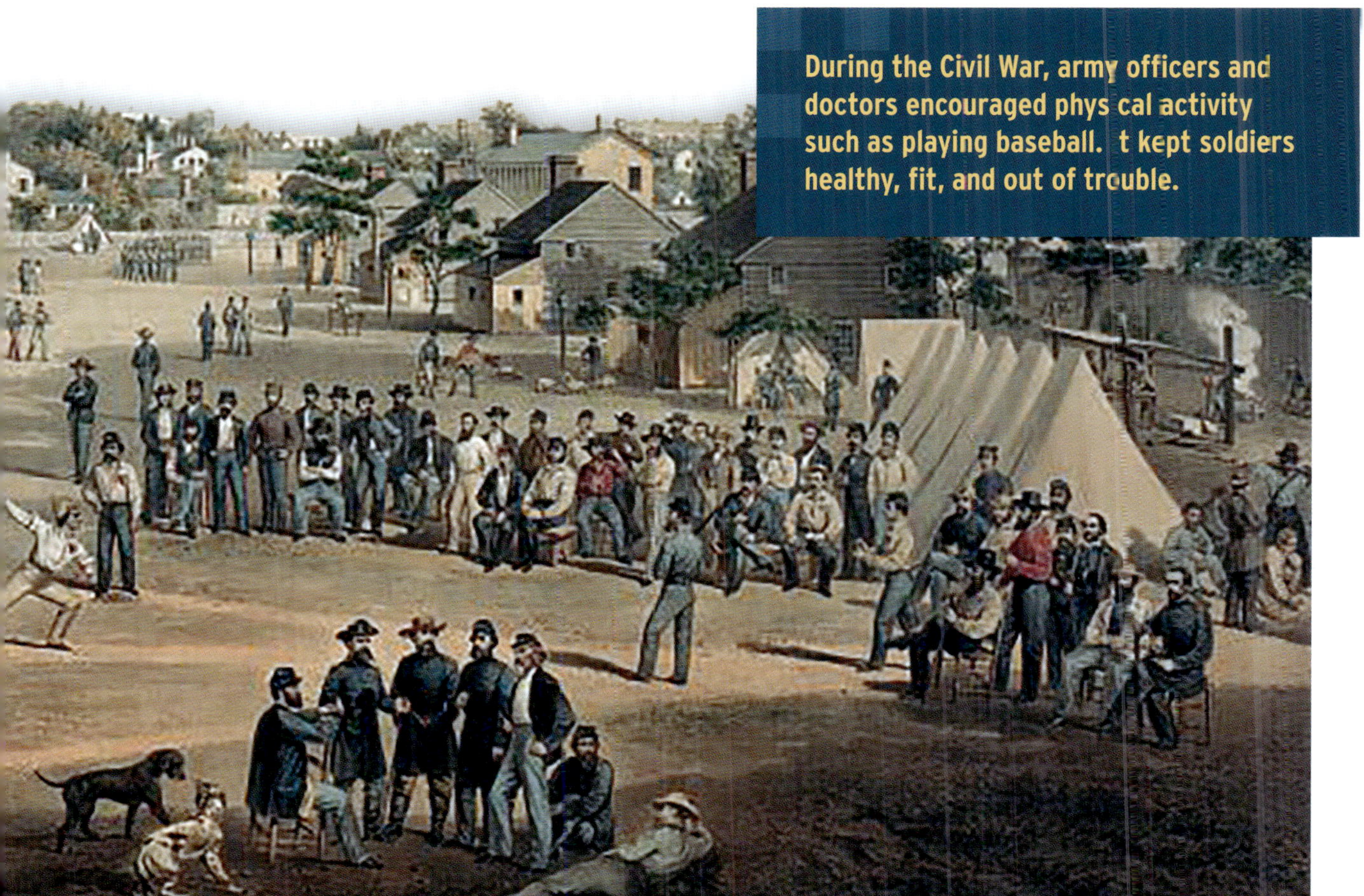

During the Civil War, army officers and doctors encouraged physical activity such as playing baseball. It kept soldiers healthy, fit, and out of trouble.

During World War II, the commissioner of baseball wrote a letter to President Franklin D. Roosevelt asking whether baseball should be suspended during the war. Roosevelt replied with a letter called the "Green Light Letter." In it, he said that professional baseball should continue. He believed it would improve morale. However, Roosevelt's legacy during World War II is not all positive.

Because Japan was one of the countries the United States was fighting, many people questioned whether Japanese Americans were loyal to the United States. Although there was no evidence that Japanese Americans were harming the war effort, Roosevelt signed an order to send them all to internment camps. The government took people

As a child, Jim Thorpe was sent to the Carlisle Indian Industrial School in Pennsylvania. He went on to play professional baseball and football and win two Olympic gold medals in track and field.

from their homes and forced them to live in poor conditions. Many died while imprisoned there. In the camps, some Japanese Americans played sports, including baseball. This helped keep their spirits up. It also showed that baseball was a sport for all Americans.

A baseball game at the Manzanar War Relocation Center in 1943. About 10,000 Japanese Americans were held in this internment camp.

Bud Fowler (*top row, third from left*) was one of the earliest known Black Americans to play professional baseball. He played for many teams between 1872 and 1904. In 2022, he was voted into the Baseball Hall of Fame.

Chapter 3

INTEGRATING BASEBALL AND AMERICA

Black Americans have played a significant role in the development of baseball in the United States. Integration was an important part of baseball's history. But it was also important to America as a whole. The integration of baseball occurred alongside integration in the rest of the country. In many ways, baseball's integration inspired integration in other parts of American life.

Players from the Start

While baseball wasn't as popular in the South before the Civil War, many people still played versions of the game. Enslaved people were among these players. After the Civil War, many Black players formed clubs and teams. But baseball associations had both official and unwritten rules of discrimination.

Despite this, some Black men were able to play professionally in the 1800s. For example, in the 1870s, Bud Fowler became one of the first Black men to play professional baseball on a team with white players. And in May 1884, Moses Fleetwood "Fleet" Walker played his first game with the Toledo Blue Stockings. This made him the first Black man to play on a Major League Baseball (MLB) team. That July, Walker's brother, Weldy Walker, joined the team as well.

In 1887, however, major and minor league team owners agreed that they would not allow Black people on their teams. By 1900, there were no Black players in America's professional leagues. But Black athletes still found ways to play the game they loved. They formed all-Black teams. The teams barnstormed around the country, playing in rural areas. These teams were a source of great pride for Black Americans.

In 1881, Fleet Walker (*middle row, left*) played for the Oberlin College baseball team with his brother Weldy Walker (*back row, second from right*).

Racism On and Off the Field

These early Black players faced a great deal of racism. For example, Fleet Walker dealt with constant discrimination, taunts, and threats while playing for Toledo. This treatment came from his own teammates, other teams, fans, and businesses in towns where the team played.

The struggles that Black players faced trying to play baseball echoed just some of the struggles Black people dealt with on a daily basis in America. At the time, segregation was not just allowed but often written into laws known as Jim Crow laws. And in 1896, the US Supreme Court declared that segregation was constitutional.

Whether it was the law or not, white Americans throughout the country discriminated openly against Black people. They believed that Black people were somehow inferior. The lack of Black players in major league baseball only reinforced this belief.

Between playing for Oberlin College and the Toledo Blue Stockings, Weldy Walker (*front row, center*) was on the University of Michigan baseball team.

The year 1920 brought about a big change for Black baseball players and for baseball itself. A Black man named Rube Foster was a manager for a barnstorming team. He saw how Black team owners and players struggled because of discrimination. Foster believed a Black professional baseball league would help Black teams. In 1920, he and other team owners formed the Negro National League (NNL). Other Black leagues soon followed.

Thanks to these leagues, star Black players were able to show white audiences their extraordinary abilities. They proved that they could compete with white players and draw crowds. Once again, baseball inspired great pride among Black Americans.

Rube Foster (*right*) was elected into the Baseball Hall of Fame in 1981.

During the Great Depression, most Black leagues disbanded.
But in 1937, the Negro American League (NAL) took the NNL's
place. The NAL continued to provide a way for some of baseball's
biggest stars to demonstrate their talents to the country. This
included one of the most famous baseball players of all time:
Jackie Robinson.

Rube Foster (*front row, third from left*) and other NNL leaders at the Negro National League annual meeting on January 28, 1922, in Chicago

Choosing a Star

Civil rights activists had been fighting for baseball's integration since the 1930s. They also advocated for integration in many other areas of American life. After Black people fought for the United States in World War II, the push became even stronger. People pointed out that it was unfair that Black men were expected to die for their country but weren't considered equal citizens.

Jackie Robinson had fought against racism his whole life, including during his time in the US Army. But he would soon face racism on a bigger stage. Branch Rickey, the general manager of the Brooklyn Dodgers, wanted to integrate baseball. In 1945, he began looking for the right Black player to be the first to play on a major league team. Rickey saw Robinson play for the Kansas City Monarchs, an NAL team. Rickey saw that Robinson was an extremely talented player. He also believed Robinson could calmly deal with the mistreatment he would face from teammates, opponents, and fans.

Before becoming the general manager of the Dodgers, Branch Rickey played for and managed the St. Louis Browns.

Jackie Robinson played for the Brooklyn Dodgers from 1947 to 1956. He was in all six All-Star Games between 1949 and 1954.

Breaking the Color Line

Robinson joined the Brooklyn Dodgers in 1947. His entry into the major leagues was a momentous occasion. It was the first time a Black man had played on an MLB team in nearly 60 years. Robinson immediately showed his skills on the field. That year he had the most stolen bases and second-most runs scored in the National League. He was chosen as the first ever Rookie of the Year.

But making this moment a reality was not easy. Robinson experienced harassment and violence from crowds. Segregation laws prevented him from staying in hotels or dining in restaurants with his teammates. Players on opposing teams attempted to injure him. Many of his own teammates protested having to play with a Black man.

Jackie Robinson was only with the Kansas City Monarchs for the 1945 season.

However, not everyone was against Robinson joining the Dodgers. He said that some players on other teams wished him well. And some of his teammates were supportive. During a game when the fans were shouting insults at Robinson, his teammate Pee Wee Reese put his arm around Robinson. Reese wanted to show the crowd that Robinson belonged on the team.

After a few years of calmly dealing with this abuse, Robinson began to speak out. He stood up for himself when he was mistreated. After he retired, he continued to stand up for his beliefs as a civil rights activist. He saw his fame as giving him a platform for fighting racism.

A Lasting Legacy

After Robinson's debut, other MLB teams started signing Black players. By 1959, all MLB teams were integrated. Black players

Jackie Robinson holding the 1949 National League Most Valuable Player Award. He was the first Black player to win it.

have had an enormous impact on baseball, from Willie Mays's amazing catch in 1954 to Hank Aaron, Barry Bonds, and Aaron Judge setting home run records. Today, Black players still do not have equal representation on baseball teams. But they continue to be signed by MLB teams and many have become baseball superstars.

The importance of Robinson's baseball career has been commemorated in many ways. In 1987, MLB renamed the Rookie of the Year award the Jackie Robinson Award. In 1997, Robinson's jersey number, 42, was retired throughout baseball's major and minor leagues. This meant the number 42 would never be assigned to another player. Robinson was the first professional athlete to have a jersey number retired across an entire sport. In 2004, MLB

In 2005, the moment between Jackie Robinson and Pee Wee Reese was memorialized as a statue in front of a minor league ballpark in Brooklyn, New York.

established Jackie Robinson Day. It is on April 15, the day of Robinson's 1947 debut with the Dodgers.

America's Color Line

Breaking the color line wasn't just momentous for baseball. It had a lasting impact on culture in the United States. Robinson's debut was essential to the civil rights movement. Martin Luther King Jr. said, "Jackie Robinson made my success possible. Without him, I would never have been able to do what I did." Former US president Barack Obama stated that Robinson "laid the foundation for America to see its Black citizens as subjects and not just objects." Baseball's integration echoed throughout the country. Other sports integrated thanks to Robinson's influence.

In 2005, US president George W. Bush (*left*) awarded Jackie Robinson the Congressional Gold Medal. Robinson died in 1972, so his wife, Rachel Robinson (*center*), accepted it in his honor.

The Honolulu Little League team celebrates after winning the 2022 Little League World Series. It was the fourth time a team from Hawaii won the tournament.

BASEBALL AND CULTURE

As America's pastime, baseball became part of American culture. It was not just a sport; it was something that nearly everyone could enjoy in one way or another. Technological and cultural developments influenced baseball, just as baseball influenced Americans' way of life. And these changes continue to impact baseball today.

Little League

Baseball has fans of all ages and genders. But professional baseball is typically played only by adult men. However, over the years, the opportunity to play baseball, whether professionally or just for fun, has opened up to a wider range of players.

Children in the United States have played baseball since before it was called baseball. Some small leagues formed in the 1880s, but they didn't last long. Kids typically played pickup games in streets or sandlots instead. These kids often didn't have good equipment. A Pennsylvania man named Carl Stotz changed that. In 1939, he established Little League, a baseball league for young boys. Local businesses sponsored the teams. This helped make it more affordable for many families to participate.

Little League grew quickly over the years. A big change came soon after the US Congress enacted a federal civil rights law called Title IX in 1972. The law made discrimination based on sex illegal in federally funded education programs. Reflecting Americans' changing values, Little League rules changed to allow girls to play starting in 1974.

Little League became a way for communities to gather and support kids. Many see it as an American tradition. Today, it is the world's largest organized youth sports program. Millions of kids ages 4 to 16 play on Little League teams around the world. Since 1947, the best teams each year have played in the Little League World Series.

Abilene, Texas, catcher Ella Bruning is one of 21 girls to play in the Little League World Series as of 2022.

All-American Girls Professional Baseball League

Women were rarely given the opportunity to play baseball. But during World War II, many baseball teams disbanded because the players were drafted into the military. To keep baseball parks in business, a women's baseball league was formed in 1943. Its name changed many times, but it is known today as the All-American Girls Professional Baseball League (AAGPBL).

The AAGPBL followed MLB rules but used underhand pitching and a softball. It also had different distances between bases and for pitching. Players were scouted from women's softball teams around the country and Canada.

The AAGPBL held to many sexist standards of the time. Players were expected to look pretty and act feminine. Their uniforms had skirts

The AAGPBL team the Racine Belles was based in Racine, Wisconsin. Players included (*left to right*) Betty Trezza, LaVonne Paire, Margaret Danhauser, Sophie Kurys, and Madeline English.

instead of pants. But the league was very successful. Since so many men had left their jobs to fight in the war, many women had started doing jobs traditionally reserved for men. This changing culture in the United States made people more accepting of women playing baseball. And the players' skill became a huge draw for fans.

The AAGPBL continued to be successful for a few years after the war ended in 1945. More than 600 women played professional baseball for the league. Eventually, men returned from the war and a new generation of boys grew up and could play professionally. The AAGPBL league disbanded. As of 2023, no woman has played on an MLB team, and there isn't an equivalent league for women. Girls often aren't allowed to play on their school teams. But the AAGPBL is a unique and inspiring part of the history of baseball and America.

Marg Callaghan of the Fort Wayne Daisies slides into home plate during the 1948 season.

Arts and Culture

Baseball has become a part of American popular culture in a way that few other sports have. Some of America's most famous authors have written about baseball. Songs have been written about the sport for more than a century. Norman Rockwell, a painter known for his works featuring American culture, created many baseball-themed paintings in the early to mid-1900s. Baseball phrases such as *hitting a home run* and *out of left field* have become part of everyday language.

Since photography was invented in the mid-1800s, photos of baseball players have been featured on trading cards. These baseball cards are a unique example of baseball influencing American culture. Originally, baseball cards were simply images of players that were sold with cigarettes to increase sales. Then kids started collecting them, so companies started selling the cards in packs of gum instead. In the 1950s,

Rare baseball cards can be very valuable. In 2021, a copy of the Honus Wagner card printed between 1909 and 1911 sold for $3.75 million!

baseball card company Topps started printing colorful, fun cards that included information about the players. Cards became increasingly valuable for many years. Today, collecting trading cards for many different sports and other activities is a popular hobby for both kids and adults.

American Heroes

Famous players have made their marks on both baseball and American culture for decades. Lou Gehrig, Joe DiMaggio, Willie Mays, Barry Bonds, Mike Trout, and more have become household names. Throughout the history of baseball, fans have collected star players' trading cards, sought their autographs, and cheered them on. But a few players' careers have had unique impacts on baseball and America.

Baseball became less popular in 1919, after eight members of the Chicago White Sox accepted money to lose the World Series. This was called the Black Sox Scandal. The scandal gave baseball a bad name, and many people stopped going to games. Around that time, Babe Ruth of the

During 12 of the seasons between 1918 and 1931, Babe Ruth hit more home runs than any other MLB player.

Boston Red Sox and later the New York Yankees started his career. His likable public image and legendary hitting drew people back to baseball. He helped save the sport.

Roberto Clemente was born in Puerto Rico. He was a star player for the Pittsburgh Pirates from 1955 to 1972. In 1973, he became the first Latin American player to be inducted into the Baseball Hall of Fame. Clemente stood up against racism and worked to help poor people in his community. He paved the way for Latin American players in MLB. Today, about one-quarter of MLB players were born in Latin America.

Babe Ruth retired in 1935 with an MLB record 714 total home runs in his career. This record stood until 1974, when Hank Aaron of the Atlanta Braves hit his 715th home run. As a Black player, Aaron faced

Hank Aaron's home run record stood until Barry Bonds (*right*) of the San Francisco Giants broke it in 2007.

racist threats by many people who didn't want him to break Babe Ruth's record. But many others supported his chase of the record. He broke it during a home game in Atlanta before a record crowd of fans.

Aaron retired two years later with 755 home runs. As of 2023, he holds the career records for total bases, runs batted in, and All-Star Games. Aaron was also known for breaking racial barriers and speaking out against racism. His baseball skills and activism helped advance civil rights in baseball and in the country.

Baseball and Technology

Technology has had a major influence on both American culture and baseball. In the early years of baseball, people had to attend the games if they wanted to know what was happening on the field in real time. But in the 1920s, baseball games began to be broadcast on the radio.

Red Barber was the announcer for the first televised baseball game, on August 26, 1939. He continued as a baseball and football sportscaster until he retired in the 1960s.

At first, few people owned radios. They gathered in public spaces to listen to the games. Soon radios became more affordable. So more people bought them and could listen to games in their homes.

In 1939, the first MLB game was televised. Television made baseball even more popular. Teams installed lights at ballparks so they could play night games. They figured more people would be home and able to watch games in the evenings.

The league made other changes to games, such as altering the rules to favor the offense. This drew more viewers who found games with a lot of hits and runs more exciting. But the availability of MLB games on the radio and television also took fans away from other leagues whose games were not broadcast. The Negro Leagues and the AAGPBL both lost fans to MLB because of technology. Technology continues to evolve and change how people watch and play baseball.

In 2022, many MLB teams started using PitchCom. The catcher uses this device to send pitch suggestions to the pitcher. The pitcher hears them through a receiver in his cap.

It's possible that MLB will start having balls
and strikes called electronically rather than
by the home plate umpires. The system was
tested in the minor leagues in 2023.

Chapter 5

WHAT'S NEXT?

As it has for more than a century, baseball continues to evolve. Star players come and go. Technology and rules change the way the game is played and enjoyed. No one can know what baseball will look like in the coming years. However, some changes are predictable and likely to occur.

Advances in Baseball and Technology

Just as radio and television broadcasts broadened baseball's fan base, streaming services have the potential to increase viewers. In 2022, viewers watched 11.5 billion minutes of baseball on MLB's streaming platform, MLB.TV. This was 10 percent more than in 2021.

New technology has affected the game too. For example, instant replay allows officials to review disputed calls. In the future, teams may use more advanced devices to record precise data on players' movements. This can help players adjust in training to improve performance or avoid injury. And computers instead of umpires may make calls during games.

A Strong Fan Base

Many people believe that baseball is on a decline, especially among younger fans and players. But the data don't support that belief. Kids continue to participate in Little League and other baseball organizations.

MLB has more attendees ages 12 to 17 than any other major professional sports league. And MLB works to keep kids interested in the sport. MLB and its players engage kids on social media platforms such as TikTok. And recent rule changes, such as the pitching timer and defensive shift limits established in 2023, are designed to make the game more fast-paced, helping to hold young fans' attention.

Women in Baseball

The AAGPBL wasn't the end of women in baseball. Today, women are growing ever closer to entering MLB. A few women play on college baseball teams and in independent professional leagues. Others coach and manage professional

MLB started allowing instant replay review in 2008. A team of umpires at MLB headquarters in New York City reviews the play and tells the result to the umpires at the game.

teams. In 2022, pitcher Kelsie Whitmore became the first woman in the starting lineup for a team in the Atlantic League, an MLB partner league.

The organization Baseball for All has helped make it possible for women to play baseball with their schools' teams and on all-women's teams. Women are likely to be a big part of baseball's future, whether their participation in school teams grows, all-women's teams and leagues develop, or they break into MLB.

A Global Game

Though baseball is a uniquely American game, it has spread to fans and players around the world. The sport is especially popular in Latin America, and most of the international players in MLB come from Latin America. Many countries have their own professional baseball leagues, including Japan, Australia, South Korea, and Cuba. In 2022, one of MLB's biggest stars was Shohei Ohtani, who started his career in Japan.

Baseball's international spread isn't slowing down anytime soon. The sport returned to the Olympics at the 2020 Summer Games in Tokyo, and it could come back in the future. Additionally, MLB is playing games overseas, particularly in London, to try to increase the sport's popularity.

Whether stars or fans are from the United States or elsewhere, thanks to the sport's uniquely American history, baseball is viewed as an American sport. Baseball is central to American culture and identity, and it likely will be for a long time to come.

What can you create that is inspired by baseball? Start by thinking about your favorite team, players, and ballpark snacks. Then put your imagination to work!

Make and decorate baseball-themed snack boxes! Then fill them with popcorn, peanuts, or another snack to munch on during a game.

Cut the leather off an old baseball and **stitch together a keychain**.

Use felt and glue-on letters to **make your own baseball pennants**. Decorate your room with them or bring them to a game to cheer on your team!

TIMELINE

1839
Abner Doubleday supposedly invents baseball. But this turns out to be a myth.

1884
Moses Fleetwood "Fleet" Walker becomes the first Black man to play for a major league team.

1861-1865
The United States fights the Civil War. Soldiers play baseball and bring a unified style home after the war.

1919
The Chicago White Sox deliberately lose the World Series for money. This becomes known as the Black Sox Scandal.

1939
Carl Stotz founds Little League. The first MLB game is televised.

1947
Jackie Robinson debuts in MLB for the Brooklyn Dodgers, breaking baseball's color line.

1920
Rube Foster and fellow baseball team owners start the Negro National League.

1943
The league now known as the All-American Girls Professional Baseball League plays its first season.

1954
Willie Mays makes "the Catch" to help the New York Giants win the World Series.

1997
Jackie Robinson's jersey number, 42, is retired throughout baseball.

1974
Hank Aaron breaks Babe Ruth's career home run record.

2022
Kelsie Whitmore becomes the first woman to pitch for an Atlantic League team.

GLOSSARY

advocate—to defend or support a cause.

assimilate—to become absorbed into a new culture or society.

atrocity—a shockingly horrible act, object, or situation.

barnstorm—to travel from place to place making brief stops to participate in a specific activity.

commemorate—to honor and remember an important person or event.

commissioner—an official in charge of an organization or government department.

constitutional—allowed according to the laws of a constitution that governs a country or state.

debut—a first appearance.

discriminate—to treat unfairly based on race, religion, gender, or other criteria. Such unfair treatment is discrimination.

draft—to select for required military service.

Great Depression—the period from 1929 to 1939 of worldwide economic trouble. There was little buying or selling, and many people could not find work.

integrate—to stop the separation of people based on race. Integration is the act of integrating.

internment—the act of confining someone, especially during a war.

legacy—something important or meaningful handed down from previous generations or from the past.

momentous—having great or lasting importance.

morale—the enthusiasm and loyalty a person or group feels about something they are involved in.

nostalgia—comforting or sentimental feelings about the past.

sandlot—a vacant lot, especially when used for unorganized sports.

segregation—the separation of an individual or a group from a larger group, especially by race.

World War II—from 1939 to 1945, fought in Europe, Asia, and Africa. Great Britain, France, the United States, the Soviet Union, and their allies were on one side. Germany, Italy, Japan, and their allies were on the other side.

Booklinks
NONFICTION NETWORK
FREE! ONLINE NONFICTION RESOURCES

To learn more about baseball, please visit **abdobooklinks.com** or scan this QR code. These links are routinely monitored and updated to provide the most current information available.

INDEX